To Sid and Denny
the best big little kids
SGT & JRE

To tFc for all the tLc
mFa

Little Kids at Home

Written by Jeffie Ross Gordon
Illustrated by Mary Ann Fraser

MODERN PUBLISHING
A Division of Unisystems, Inc.
New York, NY 10022

Table of Contents

Early in the Morning

New words for Early in the Morning

 Ethan

 Pooch

 bed

 chair

 sun

 book

 Emmy

 Father

 teddy bear

 Mother

 stairs

Early in the Morning

climbed out of ___. The morning ___ was shining.

___ was still sleeping.

___ took his ___ and tiptoed down the ___.

___ wagged his tail.

___ sat in a big ___ in the living room with his ___. ___ sat with ___ and the ___.

___ picked up a ___. "I will read this ___ to ___ and my ___," he said.

___ yawned and rested on ___ and the ___. Then ___ yawned and rested on ___.

___ and ___ and ___ came down the ___.

"___ got up early this morning," said ___.

"So did ___," said ___.

"And so did the ___," said ___.

___ and ___ and the ___ were asleep in the ___.

Getting Dressed

New words for Getting Dressed

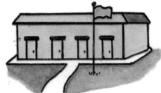 school

 dress

1 one

 socks

 shoes

2 two

 sweater

 buttons

3 three

 bears

Words you have learned

 Emmy

 Ethan

 stairs

 Mother

 Father

Getting Dressed

woke up and got ready for .

She put on her red ." **1** red ," said.

" **1** ," said . He held up **1** finger.

put on her and her ." **2** ," she said. "And

2 ."

" **2** ," said . He held up **2** fingers.

put on her green . She buttoned her . " **1** ,

2 , **3** ," she said.

" **3** ," said . He held up **3** fingers.

"Time to leave for ," called .

and ran down the .

"I counted to **3** ," said . " **1** , **2** , **3** ."

"What comes after **3** ?" asked .

" ," said . "The **3** ."

and and laughed.

New Baby

New words for New Baby

 baby

 puppy

 house

Words you have learned

 Emmy

 Pooch

 Ethan

New Baby

" , I have a surprise," said Jane.

"Me too," said Jane's brother, Scott.

"I like surprises," said .

"Me, too," said . "What is the surprise?"

"We are going to have a at our 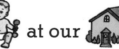 ," said Jane.

"What kind?" asked .

"Maybe it will be a girl like Jane," said .

"I don't want a girl ," said Scott.

"Maybe it will be a boy like Scott," said .

"I don't want a boy , either," said Scott.

"Then what do you want?" asked .

"I want a like  ," said Scott.

"Maybe you will get both a and a ," said .

The Best Baby Sitter

New words for The Best Baby Sitter

 books

 dinosaurs

 monkeys

 ball

 trucks

Words you have learned

 Mother

 bed

 Father

 bears

 Ethan

 Pooch

 Emmy

The Best Baby Sitter

 wore her blue skirt . "Time for work," she said.

 wore his green tie . "Time for work," he said.

"Who will stay home with and me?" asked .

"Lisa will baby-sit you," said .

"Lisa reads ," said . "She reads about and

 ."

"She reads about and ," said .

"Lisa plays with me," said .

"She tucks me into at naptime," said .

"Me, too," said .

"Woof," barked  .

"  likes Lisa, too," said .

"Lisa is the best baby sitter," said .

"The best dogsitter, too," said .

Baking Cookies

New words for Baking Cookies

 cookies

 circles

 bowl

 squares

 spoon

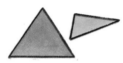 triangles

Words you have learned

 Emmy

2 two

 Ethan

Baking Cookies

"It is time to bake [cookies]," said Lisa.

"I love [cookies]," said [girl].

"Me, too," said [boy].

Lisa took out a [bowl] and a [spoon]. She mixed the [cookies].

[girl] mixed the [cookies].

[boy] also helped mix the [cookies].

[girl] cut out [cookies] shaped like [circle].

[boy] cut out [cookies] shaped like [square].

Lisa cut out [cookies] shaped like [triangle].

The [cookies] went into the oven to bake.

The [cookies] baked and cooled off. Lisa shouted, "It's time to eat the [cookies]."

[girl] ate 2 [circles]. "The [circles] are the best [cookies]," she said.

[boy] ate 2 [squares]. "The [squares] are the best [cookies]," he said.

Lisa ate 2 [triangles]. Then she ate 2 [circles] and then 2 [squares]. "I think all the [cookies] are the best," she said.

Visiting Lisa

New words for Visiting Lisa

 doll

 street

 hand

 cars

 door

 grass

Words you have learned

 Emmy

 Mother

 sweater

 Father

 book

 house

 Ethan

Visiting Lisa

"I am going to visit Lisa," said . She put on her . She took her and her .

"Can I go, too?" asked .

"Okay," said . She took his . She opened the   looked up from her . "Where are you and going?" she asked.

"We are going to visit Lisa," said .

"You're not old enough to cross the by yourself," said . "It is not safe for children because there are too many ."

"Okay, ," said . She shut the   took her and her . and 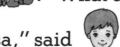 sat on the in the front yard.

 was painting the : "What are you doing?" he asked and .

"We are going to visit Lisa," said .

"You don't look like you are going anywhere," said .

"We are waiting to grow up," said .

"It is not safe for children to cross the ," said . "There are too many ."

"Well, it seems like you have grown up a little already," said .

Helping

New words for Helping

 dog house

 nails

 saw

 paint brush

 boards

 paint

 hammer

Words you have learned

 Father

 Ethan

 Pooch

 Emmy

 Mother

Helping

"Who will help me build a 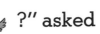 for ?" asked .

"I will help," said .

"So will I," said .

"I will help, too," said .

"I will use the ," said . "Sawing will be my job."

"I will use the ," said . "Hammering will be my job."

"I will use the ," said . "Painting the  will be my job."

"But first I must do my job," said . "It is the most important job of all."

"What's your job, ?" asked .

"I must get the 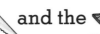 and the 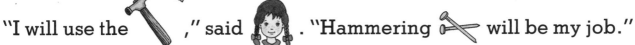 ," said . "I must buy the

and 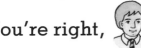 . I must buy the 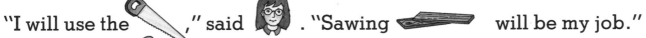 and the ."

"You're right,  ," said . "Your job is the most important."

Bathtime

New words for Bathtime

 bathtub

 pajamas

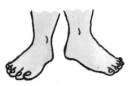 feet

 towel

 fish

Words you have learned

 Ethan

 bed

 Father

38

Bathtime

"," called . "It is bathtime."

 climbed into the . He kicked his . "I'm swimming like a ," said .

"Time for my  to get his on," said . He lifted out of the 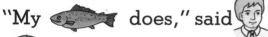.

" do not wear ," said .

"My  does," said .

 giggled as he ran to his .

"I am going to catch a ," said .

 followed into the bedroom. He dried him with a . Then he helped into his .

"How about a kiss good night?" asked .

"An kiss is better," said .

"I would like a kiss," said . "But an kiss is so much better."

Bedtime

New words for Bedtime

 rug

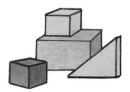 blocks

Words you have learned

 Pooch

 bed

 Ethan

 Emmy

 teddy bear

 doll

 trucks

 books

 ball

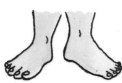 feet

 cars

 Mother

Bedtime

It was bedtime.

 was curled up on the bedroom  .

 put his and his and his and his in .

 put her and her and her in her  .

"You have a lot of toys in your  " said to and .

"We like to sleep with our toys," said .

 tucked into and then tucked into .

"Good night," said .

"Good night ," shouted and at the same time.

 wiggled his . "I don't have any room in my ," said .

 wiggled her 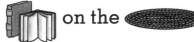 . "Me, neither," shouted .

 climbed out of his  . He put his and his on the

 . climbed out of her . She put her and her

 on the 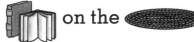 .

"Now I have room in my ," said . "Good night, ."

"Me, too," shouted . "Good night, ."

Then went to sleep on the 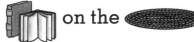 .

Words You Have Learned in Little Kids at Home

Ethan

Emmy

bed

sun

teddy bear

stairs

Pooch

chair

book

Father

Mother

school

dress

one

socks

shoes

two

sweater

buttons

three

bears

baby

house

puppy

books

monkeys

trucks

dinosaurs

ball

cookies

bowl

spoon

circles

squares

triangles

doll

door

hand

cars

grass

street

dog house

saw

boards

hammer

nails

paint

paint brush

bathtub

feet

fish

pajamas

towel

rug

blocks

3